I0815552

THROUGH THE DECADES
THE 1970s
SONY
STEREO
LOVE
IT'S THE
REAL
THING
COME
OUT
COME
OUT
BY ALICIA Z. KLEPEIS
eureka!

Eureka! books turn real stories into unforgettable experiences. This nonfiction imprint sparks curiosity, encourages critical thinking, and engages middle-grade readers. *Eureka!* books empower young minds to explore the stories of the real world, one fascinating fact at a time. Unravel the power of knowledge and lifelong learning with *Eureka!*

This edition first published in 2026 by Bellwether Media, Inc.

Library of Congress Cataloging-in-Publication Data

Names: Klepeis, Alicia, 1971- author
Title: The 1970s / by Alicia Z. Klepeis.
Description: Eureka!. | Minneapolis, Minnesota : Bellwether Media, Inc, 2026. | Series: Through the decades | Includes index. | Audience: Ages 9-15 | Audience: Grades 7-9 | Summary: "Engaging images accompany information on the 1970s. The text level and subject matter are intended for students in grades five through nine." --Provided by publisher.
Identifiers: LCCN 2025021829 (print) | LCCN 2025021830 (ebook) | ISBN 9798893045475 library binding | ISBN 9798893046854 ebook
Subjects: LCSH: United States--History--1969---Juvenile literature | United States--Civilization--20th century--Juvenile literature
Classification: LCC E169.12 .K553 2026 (print) | LCC E169.12 (ebook) | DDC 973.924--dc23/eng/20250620
LC record available at https://lccn.loc.gov/2025021829
LC ebook record available at https://lccn.loc.gov/2025021830

Editor: Christina Leaf Series Designer: Andrea Schneider Book Designer: Laura Sowers

Printed in the United States of America, North Mankato, MN.

TABLE OF CONTENTS

WELCOME TO THE 1970s!

On a rainy afternoon in 1977, a kid places the newest Queen album on the record player. He sinks into a beanbag chair on the living room floor. He starts to read the latest issue of *Cracked* magazine. Its cover is a hilarious cartoon featuring some of the *Star Wars* characters.

Later, he heads to the kitchen for a snack. He enjoys a glass of Tang and a Pillsbury Food Stick. Then, he plays Connect Four with his brother. By the time they finish, the sun is out. Suddenly, there is a knock on the door. A group of kids on the street are starting a game of Red Rover. He changes into his plaid Toughskin pants and ties his Converse All-Stars.

After the game, he heads home. He cannot wait to watch his favorite show, *The Six Million Dollar Man*. His family eats their TV dinners on tray tables close to the screen. It is a perfect night for a '70s kid!

BEANBAG CHAIR

CONVERSE ALL-STARS

TV DINNER

WHAT HAPPENED IN THE 1970s?

The 1970s is known for both social change and violence. Progress toward social change, which had flourished in the 1960s, continued in this new decade. Many **marginalized** people kept fighting for equality. Women, members of the **LGBTQ+** community, Black people, and Native American people were among them. The environmental movement also made great strides. **Activists** worked to protect the environment from many threats, including air and water pollution. New laws and policies made people safer and healthier.

Despite these advancements, the optimism of the 1960s shifted to burnout for many people. The Vietnam War and the Watergate scandal were among the causes in this change of attitude. While people focused more on broader social changes in the 1960s, they often focused on themselves in the 1970s.

Unfortunately, the 1970s saw **terrorists** around the globe use bombings, **hijackings**, kidnappings, and **assassinations** as acts of protest. These events happened in locations from the Olympics in Munich, West Germany, to a restaurant in New York City.

Following the space race of the 1960s, technology continued to boom in the 1970s. Space stations were launched into orbit for the first time. Major technological innovations occurred in the personal computing and medical fields, too.

Gloria Steinem, a women's rights and social justice activist

HOW MUCH?

1 GALLON GAS

$0.36 (1970)
$0.86 (1979)

1 GALLON MILK

$1.32 (1970)
$1.62 (1979)

THE NEW YORK TIMES

(weekday issue)

$0.15 (1970) | $0.25 (1979)

1 DOZEN EGGS

$0.62 (1970)
$0.85 (1979)

MOVIE TICKET

$1.55 (1970)
$2.47 (1979)

FIRST-CLASS STAMP

$0.06 (1970)
$0.15 (1979)

HERSHEY'S BAR

$0.10 (1970)
$0.25 (1978)

LOAF OF BREAD

$0.28 (1970)
$0.47 (1979)

HISTORY

UNITED STATES HISTORY

The Vietnam War was one of the most influential events of the 1970s. It sparked antiwar protests across the nation. Sadly, some turned deadly. On May 4, 1970, Ohio National Guard members killed four students at Kent State University.

The Vietnam War ended in 1975 but continued to affect the country. The spending on the war had hurt the American economy and led to serious **inflation**. The war also resulted in huge numbers of **casualties**.

In 1972, United States President Richard Nixon became the first American leader to visit **communist** China. The goal was improving relations between the U.S. and China. The U.S. also hoped to gain the upper hand in the **Cold War** against the **Soviet Union**. The visit was a huge success. It opened China up to the rest of the world. Nixon referred to it as "the week that changed the world."

In the late 1970s, President Jimmy Carter worked to improve human rights around the globe from Argentina to South Korea.

KENT STATE UNIVERSITY SHOOTING

VIETNAM WAR

PRESIDENT RICHARD NIXON VISITING CHINA IN 1972

JACKSON STATE UNIVERSITY KILLINGS

Tensions were high in the spring of 1970 at the historically Black Jackson State University. Students protested numerous times over their treatment by white motorists traveling through campus. But students were only socializing outside the dorms on the night of May 14–15, 1970. When police approached, someone threw a glass bottle. Officers fired into the crowd, killing two Black students.

candlelight vigil

AMERICA'S BICENTENNIAL

Across the U.S., people celebrated the nation's two-hundredth birthday in 1976. Americans were both patriotic and sentimental. Several states issued special U.S. Bicentennial license plates. Commemorative coins, posters, and stamps were popular, too. Special celebratory events included concerts, firework displays, and sporting events.

APOLLO 13

On April 11, 1970, the Apollo 13 spacecraft launched from Florida's Kennedy Space Center. This NASA mission was supposed to explore the Moon's Fra Mauro area. However, the explosion of an oxygen tank derailed its mission. Clever problem-solving led to the astronauts' safe return home on April 17.

Apollo 13 launch

UNITED STATES POLITICS

Some political agendas from the 1960s carried into the 1970s. The Environmental Protection Agency (EPA) was created in 1970. Its goals were to protect both the environment and human health. President Nixon's administration passed the Clean Air and Clean Water Acts in the early 1970s. These laws aimed to control sources of pollution.

President Jimmy Carter

ELECTION SHOWDOWN: 1976 PRESIDENTIAL ELECTION

CARTER (DEMOCRATIC)

FORD (REPUBLICAN)

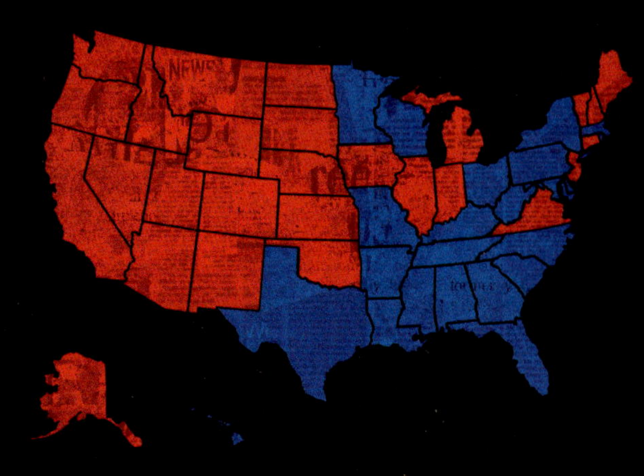

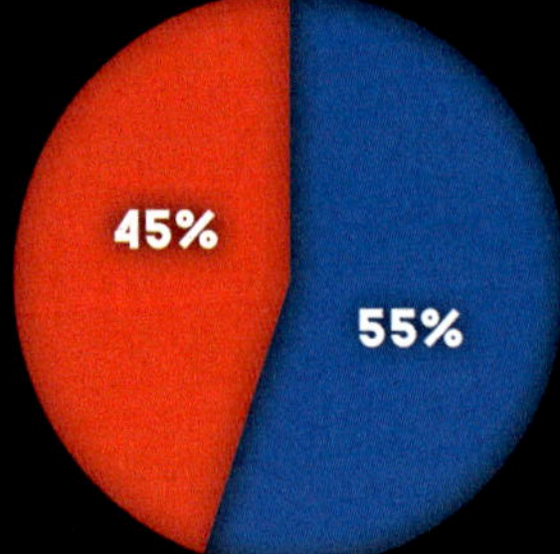

ELECTORAL VOTES

Women's rights were another important focus in 1970s American politics. The Equal Rights Amendment (ERA) was proposed in 1972. Its goal was to prevent gender from determining a person's rights. The Senate passed the ERA, but it was not **ratified** by enough states to become a law. However, the 1973 Supreme Court ruling in the *Roe v. Wade* case granted women in the U.S. a legal right to **abortion**. A 1974 law allowed women to get their own credit cards for the first time.

Despite some more progressive initiatives, a political movement called the "New Right" gained traction in the 1970s. It aimed to return to "traditional" social roles and values. Its members wanted less government interference in their lives. They fought against laws to protect the environment, raise taxes, integrate schools, and more. As the 1970s continued, Americans grew more divided politically.

YOUNGER VOTERS

The 26th Amendment to the U.S. Constitution passed in 1971. It lowered the voting age across the country from 21 to 18 years old. It was the fastest ratified amendment ever, taking 101 days.

PRESIDENT NIXON SIGNING THE CLEAN AIR ACT

RALLY SUPPORTING THE EQUAL RIGHTS AMENDMENT

ROE V. WADE

SPOTLIGHT ON:

THE WATERGATE SCANDAL

In the spring of 1972, Richard Nixon was nearing the end of his first term as U.S. President. Even though he had won the 1968 election, the **popular vote** had been very close. Nixon wanted to stay in power and was suspicious of challengers. In June 1972, police discovered five men with cameras and communications eavesdropping equipment in the Democratic National Committee office. This office was located in Washington D.C.'s Watergate complex. Later, the burglars were found to have connections to Nixon's Committee to Reelect the President. Their plan was to spy on Nixon's political opponents.

At first, the White House said Nixon had not been involved with the burglary. The media reported these statements. Nixon even won the 1972 election by a landslide. But over time, evidence mounted against Nixon. Recordings of his phone calls and conversations proved he was involved in a calculated coverup of the Watergate events. On August 8, facing the threat of **impeachment**, Nixon announced his resignation as president. With that action, his vice president, Gerald Ford, became president. Nixon is still the only U.S. president to resign.

MAKING HEADLINES

"5 Held in Plot to Bug Democrats' Office Here"

–*The Washington Post*, June 17, 1972

"NIXON TELLS EDITORS, 'I'M NOT A CROOK'"

–*THE WASHINGTON POST*, NOVEMBER 17, 1973

"Nixon Resigns"

–*The Washington Post*, August 8, 1974

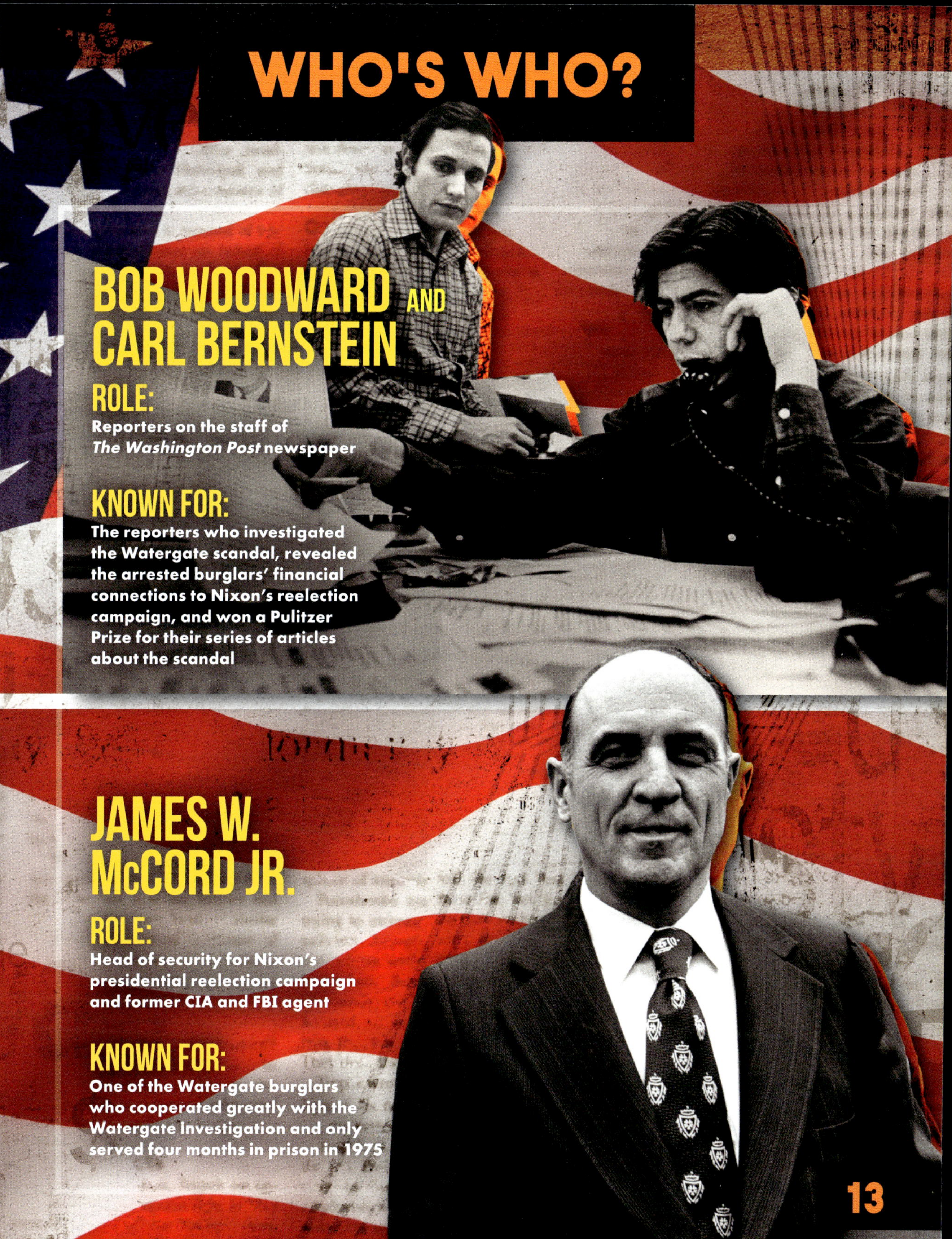

WHO'S WHO?

BOB WOODWARD AND CARL BERNSTEIN

ROLE:

Reporters on the staff of *The Washington Post* newspaper

KNOWN FOR:

The reporters who investigated the Watergate scandal, revealed the arrested burglars' financial connections to Nixon's reelection campaign, and won a Pulitzer Prize for their series of articles about the scandal

JAMES W. McCORD JR.

ROLE:

Head of security for Nixon's presidential reelection campaign and former CIA and FBI agent

KNOWN FOR:

One of the Watergate burglars who cooperated greatly with the Watergate investigation and only served four months in prison in 1975

WORLD HISTORY

Around the world, the 1970s was a decade of both creation and conflict. More than 20 new countries were established during this time. Many of them had formerly been European colonies. Examples include Angola in Africa, Fiji in Oceania, and the United Arab Emirates in Asia. Democracy also spread in Europe, as the dictatorships in Spain, Portugal, and Greece were overthrown or collapsed. Unfortunately, other nations struggled under the oppression of dictators. Pol Pot, the leader of Cambodia's Khmer Rouge government, was responsible for a brutal **genocide** from 1976 to 1979.

Much like today, there was a great deal of conflict in the Middle East in the 1970s. Arab countries and Israel had already fought three wars prior to the decade's start. In October 1973, Egypt and Syria attacked Israel in what is now known as the Yom Kippur War. Fighting stopped on October 26, but tension remained high throughout the Middle East.

ANGOLA INDEPENDENCE

POL POT

YOM KIPPUR WAR

IRAN HOSTAGE CRISIS

An uprising known as the Iranian Revolution took place from 1978 to 1979. The people established an Islamic republic. Anti-American feelings were strong. In November 1979, Iranian students took control of the American embassy in Tehran and took more than 50 Americans hostage. They remained captives for 444 days.

JIMMY CARTER AND PEACE

U.S. President Jimmy Carter played an active role in working toward peace in the Middle East. In 1978, Carter hosted the Egyptian president and Israeli prime minister at Camp David in Maryland. The conversations that took place there led to a 1979 peace treaty between Egypt and Israel.

A COOL GETAWAY

Camp David is a country retreat for U.S. presidents. The camp has a bowling alley, movie theater, hiking trails, tennis court, heated pool, and much more.

LATIN AMERICAN DICTATORSHIPS

Much of Latin America struggled under dictatorships in the 1970s. Many dictatorships were marked by the harsh treatment of political opponents. Augusto Pinochet led the military junta in Chile starting in 1973. He soon took power and ruled as a dictator. Many of his opponents were tortured. In 1976, Argentina's military dictatorship began a campaign called the Dirty War. Tens of thousands of citizens suspected of being political opponents were killed or disappeared.

Augusto Pinochet

SPOTLIGHT ON:

THE ENERGY CRISIS OF THE 1970s

In October 1973, the Organization of the Petroleum Exporting Countries (OPEC) announced that they would raise the price per barrel of oil dramatically. They also limited oil production. Although this meant that oil-producing countries would make much more money, it was a political action, too.

After the Yom Kippur War, Arab oil exporters wanted to punish countries they saw as supporting Israel. They placed an **embargo** on oil to the U.S., the Netherlands, Japan, and other countries. In the U.S., the price per barrel of oil jumped from about \$3 to almost \$12. Lines at gas stations grew longer and longer. People struggled to get the fuel they needed. This caused an energy crisis that had long-term consequences, including inflation in many nations. Following negotiations in Washington, D.C., the embargo on the U.S. was lifted in March 1974.

Some positive changes came out of the energy crisis. Countries searched for alternative energy sources. The Netherlands began to shift away from a car-based society. They built bicycle lanes and invested in public transportation. In 1977, President Jimmy Carter created the Department of Energy as one of his many environmental initiatives. He even had solar panels put on the White House roof!

MAKING HEADLINES

"OIL FLOW TO U.S. HALTED BY SAUDIS"

—*THE NEW YORK TIMES*, OCTOBER 21, 1973

"Grim Thoughts From the 'Gas' Line."

—*The New York Times*, February 19, 1974

> "Opec oil embargo leads to global fuel crisis"
>
> —*The Guardian*, November 13, 1973

> **"ARAB NATIONS LIFT OIL BAN ON DUTCH"**
>
> —***THE NEW YORK TIMES*, JULY 11, 1974**

WHO'S WHO?

HENRY KISSINGER

ROLE:
U.S. Secretary of State

KNOWN FOR:
Kissinger worked with leaders from different countries in the Middle East to resolve the conflicts from the Yom Kippur War and end the oil embargo.

SOCIAL CHANGES

The 1970s saw major changes in the workforce with more women and Black people joining. Black women began taking on more clerical work than domestic work. However, both women and Black workers only earned about 60 cents to the dollar of white men's earnings. Racial tensions grew due to frustration with these economic conditions.

The American Indian Movement fought for tribal rights during the 1970s. One big win came in 1978 with the American Indian Religious Freedom Act. This act protected the rights of Native Americans to practice their traditional religions.

More women became leaders of countries in the 1970s than ever before. Isabel Perón became the world's first woman president in 1974 in Argentina. Other countries that had women leaders in the 1970s included the Central African Republic, India, and the United Kingdom.

Harvey Milk

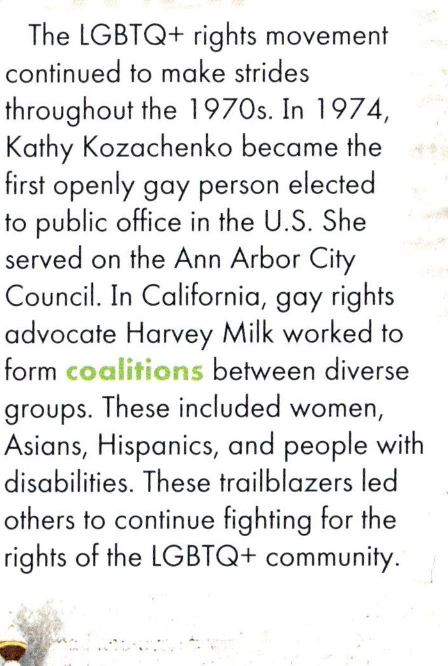

The LGBTQ+ rights movement continued to make strides throughout the 1970s. In 1974, Kathy Kozachenko became the first openly gay person elected to public office in the U.S. She served on the Ann Arbor City Council. In California, gay rights advocate Harvey Milk worked to form **coalitions** between diverse groups. These included women, Asians, Hispanics, and people with disabilities. These trailblazers led others to continue fighting for the rights of the LGBTQ+ community.

AMERICAN INDIAN MOVEMENT

KATHY KOZACHENKO

Pride flag

GAY PRIDE PARADES

On June 28, 1970, the first Pride parades in the U.S. took place in Chicago, New York City, and Los Angeles. They were held on the first anniversary of the Stonewall Uprising, when police raided a gay bar in New York City. The raid led to conflicts with police and protests that lasted six days.

ARGENTINA'S PRESIDENT ISABEL PERÓN

SCIENCE AND TECHNOLOGY

TECHNOLOGICAL ADVANCEMENTS

Many technologies we use today got their start or were dramatically improved in the 1970s. Microwaves are one example. As their parts became cheaper in the 1970s, their popularity surged. By 1975, more microwaves were sold than gas ranges.

The first digital wristwatch came out in 1972. Known as the Pulsar Time Computer, it was sleek and told the time. It cost $2,100. In today's money, that is more than $15,000!

The first generation of personal computers was sold in the 1970s. However, very few people owned them. They were expensive and had limited uses for the average person. The earliest computers did not have built-in permanent storage for data. Floppy disks held programs and stored data.

SONY WALKMAN

WHAT IS IT?:
A portable tape player

INVENTOR:
Sony co-founder Masaru Ibuka had the idea and designer Norio Ohga made the first prototype

YEAR INVENTED:
1979

EFFECT ON DAILY LIFE:
Changed the way people listen to music by allowing them to take music on the go

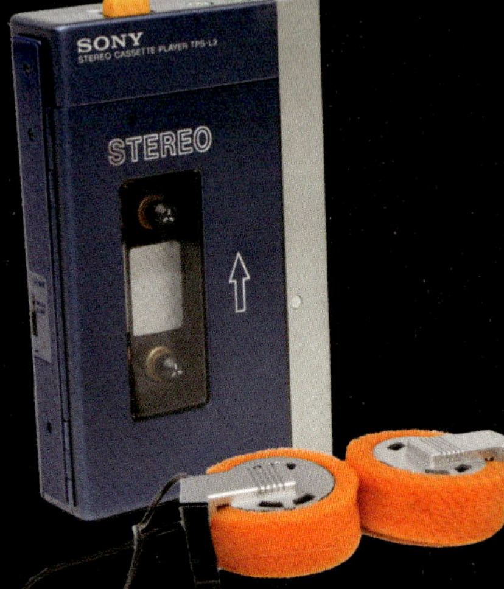

Global Positioning System (GPS) technology launched in 1978. It used the Navstar 1 satellite orbiting Earth. Originally, it was developed by the U.S. Department of Defense to help military forces navigate. Today, this technology allows people to navigate using apps such as Google Maps.

GPS SATELLITE

APPLE 1 COMPUTER

The first Apple 1 computers went on sale in 1976. But they did not come with keyboards, cases, or monitors!

Apple 1 Computer

SCIENTIFIC DISCOVERIES

The 1970s were a time of great scientific discoveries. In 1971, the Soviet Union launched the first space station to orbit Earth. NASA established its own Skylab space station in 1973. It had the first laboratory in orbit. Scientists and astronauts studied both Earth and the effects spaceflight had on peoples' bodies. NASA's Project Viking also greatly expanded our knowledge of space. Two of its probes landed on Mars, examined the chemistry of its surface, and took photos. In 1979, NASA's space probes Voyager 1 and 2 made observations of Jupiter. Their instruments gave new insight into the planet's appearance, atmosphere, and magnetic field.

Many advances were made in the medical field in the 1970s. Dr. Raymond Damadian invented the magnetic resonance imaging (MRI) scanner. This noninvasive tool allowed doctors to see inside the human body better than ever before. It also vastly improved doctors' ability to diagnose diseases such as cancer. Cancer research funded by the National Cancer Act of 1971 continued throughout the decade. After thousands of years of killing people, smallpox was **eradicated** through parts of the globe during the 1970s.

SKYLAB SPACE STATION

PHOTOS OF JUPITER FROM VOYAGER 1

DEMONSTRATION OF AN EARLY MRI SCANNER

AN UNDERGROUND ARMY

On March 29, 1974, local farmers in Xi'an, China, discovered pieces of a clay figure when digging a well. Archeologists continued the excavation and unearthed a full army of life-size terra-cotta soldiers!

DAILY LIFE

LIFE IN THE '70s

Economic struggles of the decade made daily life more difficult for many families. The gap between rich and poor widened. More families needed two parents to work outside the home to pay the bills. The number of single-parent families increased for all races.

Roughly one in four Americans lived in rural areas in the 1970s. Following the trend of the 1950s and 1960s, suburbs continued to grow, though at a slower rate. New homes also got bigger throughout the decade. Single-story ranch houses were all the rage in the 1970s. Shag carpet, wood paneling, and bold wallpaper patterns were popular ways to decorate. Station wagons were the go-to vehicle for families. People often shopped at department stores, though many were regional rather than national chains. Malls became fancier, offering live entertainment to entice shoppers and serving as popular hangout spots.

Kids in the 1970s spent much of their free time outside. They rode bikes and played games with kids who lived nearby. Indoor activities included trading baseball cards, reading comic books, and playing board games.

SINGLE-STORY RANCH HOUSE

SHAG CARPET

WALT DISNEY WORLD

Walt Disney World opened in Orlando, Florida, on October 1, 1971. About 10,000 people visited that day. Magic Kingdom was the only theme park at Walt Disney World at that time.

1970s SLANG

out to lunch
confused

catch you on the flip side
see you later

THREADS
clothes

boogie down
dance enthusiastically

Do me a solid
do me a favor

deep-six
to get rid of something

jive turkey
used mostly by Black Americans to describe someone who is dishonest or unreliable

Off The hook
very exciting

10-4
I've received your message

FASHION TRENDS

Fashion in the 1970s was fun and full of flair. Early '70s fashion was influenced by the hippie style of the previous decade. Long prairie dresses were popular. Clothing often incorporated handmade items like crochet, embroidery, and patchwork.

As the decade continued, women started to wear more comfortable clothing such as pantsuits. Both men and women started to wear jeans more. Bell-bottom pants were quite trendy. Wrap dresses became a wardrobe essential for many women, as they could be worn from work to a night out.

MOOD RINGS

Mood rings were a fashion fad in the 1970s. Liquid crystals that changed color with temperature were inside the rings. Each color was said to reflect a different mood for the wearer.

bell-bottoms

Many refer to the 1970s as the "Polyester Decade" because **synthetic** fabrics were fashionable and affordable. Men commonly sported colorful, casual suits called leisure suits made of polyester. Both girls and boys often wore plaid polyester pants.

Disco influenced this era's fashion. Dancers across the U.S. sported sequins, satin, and hot pants. Women and men wore platform shoes with thick soles and chunky heels.

The 1970s were known for some iconic hairstyles. Celebrities like Diana Ross wore Afros for style and political reasons. *Charlie's Angels* actress Farrah Fawcett was famous for her feathered hairstyle. Rockers David Bowie and Mick Jagger sported the layered shag style.

YELLOW LEISURE SUIT

DISCO FASHION

Farrah Fawcett

DIANA ROSS WEARING AN AFRO

PRODUCTS AND TOYS

Most toys in the 1970s did not need a power source. Action figures, board games, dolls, toy trucks, and outdoor toys were all the rage. But as the decade ended, some electronic toys became popular, including the first at-home gaming consoles!

BABY ALIVE

Kenner introduced Baby Alive in 1973. Children could give this doll a bottle of liquid and special food packets. The doll would pee and poop in her diaper. Customers could buy a white or Black Baby Alive doll.

ATARI 2600 VIDEO COMPUTER SYSTEM

The Atari 2600 Video Computer System was the home gaming console of choice. It came out in 1977 and was known for its sharp sound and colorful graphics. Initially there were nine games available including *Combat, Street Racer,* and *Blackjack*.

STAR WARS ACTION FIGURES

A series of *Star Wars* action figures came out after the release of the blockbuster film in 1977. Fans could not wait to get their hands on these small plastic figures. Han Solo, Luke Skywalker, and Chewbacca were just a few options.

PET ROCK

The Pet Rock was a collectible toy first introduced in 1975. Each rock came in a special cardboard box that had straw bedding and ventilation holes like a real pet carrier. Kids bought more than a million of this toy.

BOGGLE

Boggle is a fun game first marketed by Parker Brothers in 1972. It features a grid of 16 dice with letters on them. Players have three minutes to come up with as many words as they can.

MATTEL ELECTRONICS FOOTBALL

In 1977, Mattel unveiled a portable gaming device called Mattel Electronics Football. Players tried to move the running back around bright red defenders. Then, they tried to score! This popular game led the way for more portable gaming devices in the 1980s.

NERF FOOTBALL

The Nerf Football debuted in 1972. Fred Cox, a kicker for the Minnesota Vikings team, came up with the idea for this lighter sports ball to prevent kids from getting sore legs and arms.

GREEN MACHINE

Marx Toys released the Green Machine in the late 1970s. This three-wheeled cruiser was made mainly of colorful plastic. It had a big front wheel and swivel-action rear wheels. Its stick shift controls allowed for turning, twisting, and spinning out.

ARTS AND ENTERTAINMENT

PUBLICATIONS

The 1970s were a groundbreaking decade when it came to reading materials. Writer Tom Wolfe referred to the 1970s as the "'Me' Decade." Self-help books and articles were at their peak along with books that opened up frank discussions of sexuality, race, and women's roles in a changing society. Thanks in part to best-selling author Stephen King, horror novels also grew in popularity during the 1970s.

Readers of all ages and interests could find a magazine that appealed to them. Athletically-minded readers could enjoy monthly issues of new magazines like *Black Sports* or *Backpacker*. Comic book lovers could get lost in the debut of *Luke Cage, Power Man* or Jack Kirby's *Black Panther*. The Black superhero Storm thrilled female readers when she appeared in the 1975 issue *Giant-Size X-Men* #1.

READING REC

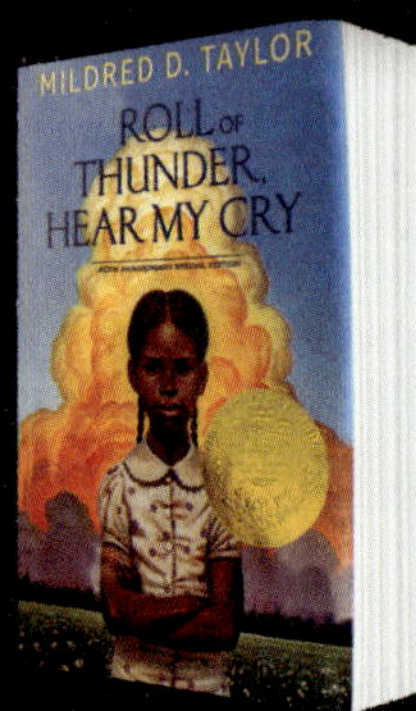

TITLE:
ROLL OF THUNDER, HEAR MY CRY

AUTHOR:
Mildred D. Taylor

YEAR PUBLISHED:
1976

SUMMARY:
The story follows Cassie, a Black girl living in Mississippi in the 1930s. Cassie begins to notice how Black children are treated differently than white children. This discrimination along with acts of racism show Cassie why her family's land is so important to them.

Gloria Steinem On Sisterhood
Letty Pogrebin On Raising Kids Without Sex Roles
Ms.
Sylvia Plath's Last Major Work
Women Tell The Truth About Their Abortions
THE NEW MAGAZINE FOR WOMEN
Jane O'Reilly on The Housewife's Moment of Truth

MS. MAGAZINE

Female activists Gloria Steinem and Dorothy Pittman Hughes founded *Ms.* magazine. Its first issue came out on July 1, 1972, and featured Wonder Woman on the cover. Its articles focused on women's rights and the feminist movement. The magazine was a huge departure from most women's magazines of the time, which focused on topics like homemaking and cosmetics.

Katherine Paterson

BRIDGE TO TERABITHIA

Katherine Paterson's novel *Bridge to Terabithia* came out in 1977. It has become a classic for young readers for many reasons. It shows a strong friendship between a boy and a girl. It also addresses the topic of grief well. It won the Newbery Medal in 1978.

WHERE THE SIDEWALK ENDS

Shel Silverstein's *Where the Sidewalk Ends* is a children's poetry collection released in 1974. Some poems tell whimsical, imaginative stories. Others explore weightier themes like growing up or the relationship between humans and nature. Some adults considered the book's humor to be inappropriate. Despite being banned by some libraries, the book is considered a classic today.

JUDY BLUME

Judy Blume was a wildly successful children's author in the 1970s. Her books, including the beloved *Tales of a Fourth Grade Nothing*, are known for their humor. Her 1970 novel *Are You There, God? It's Me, Margaret* was somewhat radical in its frankness. Young readers could relate to the main character Margaret's experiences going through puberty.

Judy Blume

MOVIES

Long before people streamed films at home, going to the movies was a favorite form of 1970s entertainment. A new invention called the Steadicam allowed film crews to shoot in many more locations without any shakiness. This technology was used in iconic '70s movies including *Rocky* and *The Shining*. Francis Ford Coppola and Martin Scorsese made intense, gritty films such as *The Godfather* and *Taxi Driver*. This rough-edged style marked a change from earlier decades. Previously, a set of rules called the Hays Code banned things such as offensive words and violence in movies. Starting in 1968, movie ratings suggested whether films were deemed appropriate for different-aged viewers.

In 1976, video home system (VHS) tapes became available to consumers. This changed the way people watched films. They could now watch movies at home!

VHS tapes

AT THE BOX OFFICE

TOP-GROSSING FILMS OF THE 1970s

- ***Star Wars*** **(1977)**
- ***Jaws*** **(1975)**
- ***The Exorcist*** **(1973)**
- ***Enter the Dragon*** **(1973)**
- ***Grease*** **(1978)**
- ***Close Encounters of the Third Kind*** **(1977)**
- ***Superman*** **(1978)**
- ***Smokey and the Bandit*** **(1977)**
- ***The Godfather*** **(1972)**
- ***Saturday Night Fever*** **(1977)**

Grease

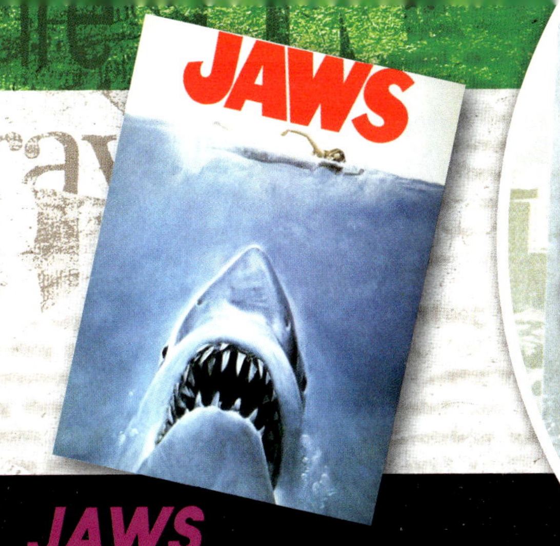

JAWS

Released on June 20, 1975, *Jaws* is regarded as the first summer blockbuster. Steven Spielberg directed this Oscar-winning movie about a killer shark terrorizing a small town. It became the first film ever to earn over $100 million in U.S. theaters.

DISASTER MOVIES

The disaster movie was a genre that boomed in the 1970s. *Airport*, a dramatic air disaster film released in 1970, started the trend. It was the first in a series of four Airport films. Other disaster movies included the 1974 releases of *The Towering Inferno* and *Earthquake*.

Earthquake

LOTS OF CHOCOLATE

A favorite kids' movie of the 1970s was *Willy Wonka and the Chocolate Factory*. The chocolate river in the film contained a powder used in making chocolate ice cream. But after weeks of filming, it went bad and turned the river stinky!

STAR WARS

No discussion of 1970s movies would be complete without George Lucas's *Star Wars*. Released in 1977, this epic saga has spurred sequels and prequels that stretched well into the new millennium. Its actors, including Harrison Ford and Mark Hamill, became household names. The film won six Academy Awards!

VIDEO RENTAL STORES

When the first movies were released on VHS tapes, they were very expensive to buy. People often went to video rental stores to check out a film for a night. The first video rental store opened in Los Angeles in 1977. People paid $50 for an annual membership. They could then rent a movie for $10 per night, equivalent to over $54 in today's money!

TELEVISION AND RADIO

In the 1970s, the NBC, ABC, and CBS networks dominated what was on television. Hardly anyone had cable TV. People watched what was on when it aired.

More than in previous decades, networks aimed to appeal to younger viewers. There was also a push for more **diversity** in both the audience and the programming, thanks to the Civil Rights Movement. Game shows and soap operas often aired during the day. But millions of viewers tuned into their favorite sitcoms at night. Musical variety shows were popular at the start of the decade but faded by its end.

Right up through the 1960s, most Americans listened to AM radio stations. Talk shows were common. During the 1970s, FM stations became dominant. The FM band offered listeners better sound quality and a wide variety of music genres.

SATURDAY NIGHT LIVE

The late-night comedy show *Saturday Night Live,* known widely as *SNL,* debuted in 1975. Its edgy humor was designed to attract viewers from ages 18 to 34. Producer Lorne Michaels has broadcast the series live since its start. Satirical sketches and performances by musical guests have entertained audiences ever since.

MINISERIES

Miniseries based on novels became a hugely popular new genre with TV audiences starting in the mid-1970s. ABC aired *Rich Man, Poor Man* in 1976. The historical drama *Roots* aired on ABC over eight nights in 1977. It looked at the slave trade and slavery in America. Despite its weighty subject matter, it drew in more viewers in the U.S. than any other program of the decade.

SOUL TRAIN

Soul Train was a groundbreaking Black music and dance program. It first aired in Chicago in 1970 but was shown across the U.S. starting in 1971. Dancers lined up to show off their moves on TV. The program also provided a platform for Black artists, including the Jackson 5 and Aretha Franklin, to showcase their work. The show was a can't-miss event for many Black people.

ALL IN THE FAMILY

In 1971, *All in the Family* premiered on CBS. The groundbreaking show addressed a range of political and social issues. These included women's rights, racism, and poverty. The show used humor as a way to broach subjects that were previously avoided on TV sitcoms. It also led to several very successful spinoff shows such as *Maude, Good Times,* and *The Jeffersons.*

CHILDREN'S PROGRAMMING

Kermit the Frog

The 1970s saw a boom in quality television shows geared at children. Following educational programs like *Sesame Street* and *Mister Rogers' Neighborhood, The Electric Company* premiered in 1971 on PBS. Entertained by puppets and famous guest stars alike, families first tuned in to *The Muppet Show* in 1976. Family-friendly sitcoms included *The Brady Bunch* and *The Partridge Family. Schoolhouse Rock!,* a series of educational cartoon shorts, aired between Saturday morning cartoons.

MUSIC

When it came to music, the 1970s was a time of extraordinary creativity. Solo artists such as Elton John and David Bowie gave flashy performances. Hip-hop artists including the Sugarhill Gang and Kurtis Blow became wildly popular. Disco music soared to the top of the pop charts as the 1970s continued. The smooth vibe of soft rock remained a radio favorite throughout the decade.

Most people in the 1970s bought their music on vinyl, including "mini" record singles called 45s. Some cars had 8-track cartridge players or cassette players, which grew in popularity in the late 1970s. People listened to cassettes in portable Walkman players at the end of the decade.

CLIMBING THE CHARTS

In 1974, the band Redbone made history with their song "Come and Get Your Love." They were the first all Native and Mexican American band to reach the Top 5 on the *Billboard* chart. The band's founders, Lolly and Pat Vegas, have Yaqui and Shoshone heritage.

1970s PLAYLIST

- ***Blitzkrieg Bop*** **The Ramones (1976)**
- ***Born to Run*** **Bruce Springsteen (1975)**
- ***Dancing Queen*** **ABBA (1976)**
- ***Dreams*** **Fleetwood Mac (1977)**
- ***I Will Survive*** **Gloria Gaynor (1978)**
- ***Midnight Train To Georgia*** **Gladys Knight & the Pips (1973)**
- ***Night Fever*** **Bee Gees (1977)**
- ***Philadelphia Freedom*** **Elton John (1977)**
- ***Rhymin' and Rappin'*** **Paulette & Tanya Winley (1979)**
- ***Superstition*** **Stevie Wonder (1972)**

45s

John Travolta in *Saturday Night Fever*

PUNK

Although it began in some locations in the 1960s, punk rock really hit its height in the 1970s. It was known for being loud, fast, and wild. A spirit of rebellion united punk artists, not only in their music, but in their appearance and behavior, too. The Clash was a popular British punk band. The Stooges and The Ramones were American punk innovators.

The Ramones

DISCO

Disco music is known for its danceable, up-tempo beats. Initially, disco musicians, dancers, and fans were Black and Hispanic. Disco culture also offered connection and self-expression to the LGBTQ+ community. The movie *Saturday Night Fever* helped disco spread into the mainstream. Popular disco artists included the Bee Gees, Donna Summer, and the Village People.

SOFT ROCK

Soft rock dominated the airwaves in the 1970s. Popular bands included Fleetwood Mac, the Eagles, and the Carpenters. Solo artists included Barry Manilow, Neil Diamond, and Anne Murray. As a genre, soft rock is known for its pop hooks and quality studio production.

HIP-HOP

Hip-hop began to spread in 1973 at parties in the Bronx in New York City. It was characterized by spinning records on turntables, scratching, and extending percussion breaks. DJ Kool Herc was one of the pioneers of hip-hop music, helping to create and spread this new sound. Later, **MCs** started to freestyle over the music, beginning rap.

THE HUSTLE

In July 1975, singer Van McCoy's "The Hustle" hit the top of the *Billboard* Hot 100. It topped the Hot Soul Singles chart at the same time. The dance associated with this song sparked a huge dance craze. It was a blend of Latin and swing dancing. Variations included the Line, the Latin, and the New York.

U.S. SPORTS

Many U.S. professional sports leagues expanded in the 1970s. New **franchises** were added to the major professional football, basketball, baseball, and ice hockey leagues.

In some sports, a few teams dominated the decade. From 1972 to 1974, the Oakland Athletics won three consecutive World Series in Major League Baseball (MLB). In the National Football League (NFL), the Pittsburgh Steelers won three Super Bowls. But the National Hockey League's (NHL) Montreal Canadiens were the super champs. They won the Stanley Cup a whopping six times in the 1970s!

Several records were broken in the 1970s. The Miami Dolphins had a perfect season in 1972, going 17-0. No other NFL team has ever done that! In 1974, Hank Aaron hit his 715th home run. That broke Babe Ruth's home run record from 1935.

MVP

NAME:
JACK NICKLAUS

SPORT:
Golf

YEARS PLAYED:
1962 to 2005

KNOWN FOR:
Considered the best golfer of the 1970s, Nicklaus won eight major titles during the decade. He was also named PGA Player of the Year four times between 1972 and 1976.

FAMILY GOALS

In 1973–1974, the Howe family made hockey history. Gordie Howe and his sons, Mark and Marty, all played on the same World Hockey Association team, the Houston Aeros.

Billie Jean King

BATTLE OF THE SEXES

On September 20, 1973, a tennis match known as the "Battle of the Sexes" took place. Nearly 90 million people tuned in worldwide to watch this match. It was a key moment for women's rights and sports. Billie Jean King beat former number one men's player Bobby Riggs. Riggs had been boasting and criticizing women's tennis.

Julius Erving

AMERICAN BASKETBALL ASSOCIATION

The American Basketball Association (ABA) was a popular rival league to the National Basketball Association (NBA). It was known for its creative style of play and introducing the 3-point shot. Julius Erving, also known as Dr. J, was a famous ABA player. This league merged with the NBA beginning with the 1976–1977 season.

TITLE IX

In 1972, a civil rights law called Title IX passed in the U.S. It banned gender discrimination for any educational program or activity that receives money from the government. This law caused a big change in athletics. Before the law passed, girls and women did not have the same opportunities to play on sports teams. More than ten times as many girls participate in sports now than when Title IX passed.

HORSE RACING

The Triple Crown is the ultimate achievement in American horse racing. It occurs when a Thoroughbred horse wins the Kentucky Derby, the Preakness Stakes, and the Belmont Stakes in one season. Three happened in the 1970s, with Secretariat winning in 1973, Seattle Slew in 1977, and Affirmed in 1978.

MUHAMMAD ALI

Muhammad Ali brought much attention to the sport of boxing in the 1970s. In October 1974, he beat defending champion George Foreman in a famous fight called the "Rumble in the Jungle." It took place in Kinshasa in today's Democratic Republic of the Congo. Nicknamed "The Greatest," Ali was the first boxer to win the world heavyweight championship three times.

GLOBAL SPORTS

Amazing athletic competitions and feats took place throughout the 1970s. Many new sports were introduced at the Olympic Games, including numerous women's sports. Sadly, terrorist violence marred the 1972 Olympics in Munich, West Germany. Members of a Palestinian militant group attacked Israeli athletes. Eleven members of the Israeli team died in the attack.

Soccer fans were thrilled to watch the first FIFA World Cup broadcast on color television in 1970. This was the first World Cup held in North America as well as the first to use red and yellow cards. Whether in sports or science, the 1970s was a decade worth remembering!

OLYMPIC BOYCOTT

Over 20 African countries boycotted the 1976 Summer Olympic Games in Montreal, Canada. Tanzania organized this boycott to protest New Zealand's participation in the Games. New Zealand's rugby team had toured and competed in South Africa. Other countries were angry that this legitimized South Africa and its **apartheid** laws.

ARTHUR ASHE

On July 5, 1975, Arthur Ashe made tennis history when he won his match against Jimmy Connors. Ashe became the first Black man to ever win Wimbledon, one of the four Grand Slam tournaments. In 1997, the United States Tennis Association named its new stadium after this legendary player.

SPECIAL OLYMPICS WINTER GAMES

The Special Olympics held its first Winter Games in 1977 in Steamboat Springs, Colorado. It consisted of skating and skiing events. Over 500 athletes competed!

Olgo Korbut

Pelé

BRAZIL'S HISTORIC WIN

At the 1970 FIFA World Cup final, soccer fans were thrilled to watch Pelé lead Brazil to victory over Italy. This was the global superstar's fourth and final World Cup. The team's win made Brazil the first to win three World Cups.

WOMEN'S GYMNASTICS

Great strides were made in women's gymnastics in the 1970s. In 1972, Belarusian gymnast Olga Korbut won three gold medals for her performances in the Olympics. Her strength and dramatic acrobatic skills, like the Korbut flip, changed how people think about the sport. In 1976, Romanian gymnast Nadia Comăneci was the first to earn a perfect score of 10 at the Olympics.

TIMELINE

APRIL 22, 1970
Earth Day is celebrated for the first time in the U.S.

MAY 4, 1970
Four students are killed during an antiwar protest at Ohio's Kent State University

DECEMBER 2, 1970
President Richard Nixon creates the Environmental Protection Agency (EPA)

APRIL 19, 1971
The Soviet Union launches Salyut, the world's first space station orbiting Earth

FEBRUARY 21, 1972
President Richard Nixon is the first U.S. president to visit China

JUNE 17, 1972
Police arrest five burglars at the Watergate complex's Democratic National Committee headquarters, starting what will become known as the Watergate scandal

SEPTEMBER 5, 1972
A terrorist attack at the Munich Olympics leaves 11 members of Israel's Olympic team, 5 members of the Palestinian terrorist group Black September, and 1 West German policeman dead

JANUARY 22, 1973
The Supreme Court rules that women have the right to have an abortion in the *Roe v. Wade* case

JANUARY 27, 1973

With the signing of the Paris Peace Accords, the U.S. formally ends its participation in the Vietnam War

OCTOBER 1973

The Arab oil embargo takes effect, stopping oil shipments from the Middle East to the U.S. and a few other nations

OCTOBER 6, 1973

Egypt and Syria attack Israel, beginning the Yom Kippur War

MARCH 1974

The Arab oil embargo on the U.S. is lifted

MARCH 29, 1974

Farmers in Xi'an, China, discover fragments of an army of life-sized terra-cotta soldiers

APRIL 2, 1974

Kathy Kozachenko becomes the first openly gay person elected to political office in the U.S.

JULY 1, 1974

In Argentina, Isabel Perón becomes the world's first woman president

AUGUST 8, 1974
Richard Nixon announces his resignation, becoming the first U.S. President to resign from office

JULY 4, 1976
Cities across the U.S. celebrate the country's bicentennial and the two-hundredth anniversary of when the Declaration of Independence was adopted

NOVEMBER 2, 1976
Jimmy Carter wins the U.S. presidential election, defeating incumbent President Gerald Ford

JULY 5, 1975
Arthur Ashe becomes the first Black man to win Wimbledon

APRIL 1, 1976
Steve Jobs and Steve Wozniak found Apple Computer, Inc.

JANUARY 30, 1977
About 100 million Americans tune into the final night of the *Roots* miniseries

APRIL 30, 1975
Saigon, South Vietnam's capital city, falls to the North Vietnamese Army, ending the Vietnam War

JULY 20, 1976
NASA's Viking 1 space probe lands on the surface of Mars

SEPTEMBER 11, 1977

The Atari 2600 Video Computer System is released for sale

JULY 1, 1979

The Sony Walkman goes on sale, offering listeners a portable music source

MAY 25, 1977

The film *Star Wars* opens in theaters across the U.S.

MARCH 28, 1979

A partial meltdown occurs at the Three Mile Island nuclear power plant in Pennsylvania

SEPTEMBER 17, 1978

Following a summit with U.S. President Jimmy Carter, Egyptian President Anwar Sadat and Israeli Prime Minister Menachem Begin sign the Camp David Accords

AUGUST 16, 1977

Elvis Presley, also known as the "King of Rock and Roll," dies at age 42

NOVEMBER 4, 1979

A group of Iranian militants takes over the U.S. Embassy in Tehran, taking 66 American hostages

GLOSSARY

abortion—the ending of a pregnancy

activists—people who believe in taking action to make changes in laws or society

apartheid—a policy that separated and discriminated against people based on their race

assassinations—murders done in surprise attacks, commonly for political reasons

casualties—people injured or killed in either a war or accident

coalitions—alliances of distinct people, parties, or states formed for group action

Cold War—a conflict between the U.S. and the Soviet Union in the second half of the 1900s that did not break out into fighting

communist—related to communism; communism is a social system in which property and goods are controlled by the government.

discrimination—the act of treating someone unfairly because of race, gender, age, or other differences

diversity—having a variety of people or things from many different backgrounds

embargo—a legal ban on trade or other commercial activity with a specific country

eradicated—ended or destroyed completely

franchises—teams that are members of a professional sports league

genocide—the deliberate and systematic destruction of racial, political, or cultural groups

genre—a category of a kind of art based on style, form, or content

hijackings—acts in which an aircraft, ship, or vehicle are unlawfully seized while in transit

impeachment—the charging of a public official, such as the president, with a crime or misconduct

inflation—a general increase in the prices of goods and a drop in the purchasing power of money

junta—a small group, often made up of military officers, that takes power over a country by force

LGBTQ+—a community of people who identify as something other than heterosexual or the gender they were assigned at birth; LGBTQ+ stands for Lesbian, Gay, Bisexual, Transgender, Queer and other identities.

marginalized—referring to people or a group of people who are treated as unimportant or outside the mainstream of society

MCs—rappers

millennium—a period of a thousand years

popular vote—the votes cast by qualified voters among the general population

racism—the belief that race is a fundamental part of human traits and that certain races are superior to others

ratified—signed or gave formal consent to an agreement, treaty, or contract, making it officially valid

satirical—using sarcasm or irony to mock behavior, beliefs, or institutions

Soviet Union—short for the Union of Soviet Socialist Republics; the Soviet Union is a former country in Eastern Europe and western Asia made up of 15 republics or states that broke up in 1991.

synthetic—not natural; produced by people using chemical means.

terrorists—people who use fear to try to control others

WRITE ABOUT IT!

- If you could go back in time to the 1970s, which elements of daily life would be most appealing to you and **why**?
- What technological advances do you think 1970s inventors and scientists would be most surprised by? **Why**?
- **Where** do you see parallels between the 1970s and today? Choose one and draw comparisons between the two.

ALSO CHECK OUT

INDEX

The images in this book are reproduced through the courtesy of: Department of Defense/ Wikipedia, front cover (Carter); INTERFOTO/ Alamy Stock Photo, front cover (Sony Walkman), p. 45 (Sony Walkman); Keystone Press/ Alamy Stock Photo, front cover (Billie Jean King), pp. 14 (Independence), 43 (July 1974); Ed Kolenovsky/ AP Images, front cover (fight); Yearling/ Wikipedia, front cover (book); CBS Television Network/ Wikipedia, front cover (The Jeffersons); PA Images/ Alamy Stock Photo, front cover (protest); Bettmann/ Getty Images, pp. 3 (Skylab), 5 (watching TV), 18-19 (Harvey Milk), 22 (Skylab, MRI), 39 (Billie Jean King), 39 (Muhammad Ali), 40 (Winter 1976); H. Armstrong Roberts/ ClassicStock/ Getty Images, pp. 3 (Roe v. Wade), 11 (Roe v. Wade); RGR Collection/ Alamy Stock Photo, pp. 3 (Star Wars), 27 (Fawcett), 32 (Jaws), 33 (Star Wars); Central Press/ Getty Images, pp. 3 (Arthur Ashe), 41 (Ashe); Retro AdArchives/ Alamy Stock Photo, pp. 4 (The Six Million Dollar Man); Christina Leaf, pp. 4 (Queen album), 36 (45s); nikkytok, p. 4 (beanbag chair); Luca, p. 4 (Converse All-Stars); CSA Images, p. 5 (TV dinner); Jay Godwin/ Wikipedia, p. 6 (Steinem); Winai Tepsuttinun, p. 7 (gas); Photo Builder, p. 7 (newspaper); tab62, p. 7 (eggs); phive2015, p. 7 (bread); Hajrudin, p. 7 (Hershey's bar); John Filo/ Wikipedia, p. 8 (shooting); U.S. Air Force, p. 8 (Vietnam War); Stringer/ Getty Images, p. 8 (president); Chermayeff and Geismar/ Wikipedia, p. 9 (bicentennial); Jackson State University/ Getty Images, p. 9 (killings); NASA/ Wikipedia, pp. 9 (Apollo 13), 22 (Jupiter); ZUMA Press, Inc./ Alamy Stock Photo, p. 10; White House Photo Office/ Wikipedia, p. 11 (signing); Florida Memory/ Wikipedia, p. 11 (rally); The Washington Post/ Getty Images, p. 13 (Woodward, Bernstein); ASSOCIATED PRESS/ AP Images, p. 13 (McCord, Jr.); CPA Media Pte Ltd/ Alamy Stock Photo, p. 14 (Pol Pot); Album/ Alamy Stock Photo, p. 14 (war); CIA/ Wikipedia, p. 15 (peace); Pictorial Press Ltd/ Alamy Stock Photo, pp. 15 (hostage), 32 (earthquake); Ministerio de Relaciones Exteriores de Chile/ Wikipedia, p. 15 (Pinochet); Consolidated News Pictures/ Getty Images, p. 17; Martin Wahlborg, p. 19 (flag); Buddy Mays/ Getty Images, p. 19 (AIM); Bloomberg/ Getty Images, p. 19 (Kozachenko); World History Archive/ Alamy Stock Photo, p. 19 (Perón); Chris Willson/ Alamy Stock Photo, pp. 20, 28 (Atari 2600, action figures); U.S. Navy/ Wikipedia, p. 21 (GPS); MediaNews Group/ Bay Area News via Getty Images/ Getty Images, p. 21 (computer); Vichaya Kiatying-Angsulee/ Alamy Stock Photo, p. 23; Camerique/ Alamy Stock Photo, p. 24 (house); ClassicStock/ Alamy Stock Photo, p. 24 (carpet); Moodman001/ Wikipedia, p. 26 (ring); Jack Kay/ Getty Images, pp. 26-27 (bell-bottoms); Fortepan/ Wikipedia, p. 27 (leisure suit); David Redfern/ Getty Images, p. 27 (disco); Harry Langdon/ Getty Images, p. 27 (Ross); stockyme, p. 29 (Boggle); NERF/ Wikipedia, p. 29 (Nerf); Dan Hardy/ AP Images, p. 29 (Pet Rock); Iain Masterton/ Alamy Stock Photo, p. 29 (Mattel Electronic Football); Rebecca Sabelko, p. 30 (book); Liberty Media for Women, LLC, p.31 (Ms. magainze); Leigh Vogel/ Getty Images, p. 31 (Katherine Paterson); Evening Standard/ Getty Images, p. 31 (Judy Blume); solidmaks, p. 32 (VHS); Universal Images Group North America LLC/ Alamy Stock Photo, p. 32 (Grease); steheap, p. 34 (radio); PictureLux/ The Hollywood Archive/ Alamy Stock Photo, pp. 34 (SNL), 45 (1977); Soul Train/ Getty Images, p. 35 (Soul Train); Allstar Picture Library Limited./ Alamy Stock Photo, p. 35 (All In The Family); Pattie/ Wikipedia, p. 35 (Kermit); United Archives GmbH/ Alamy Stock Photo, p. 36 (Redbone); FlixPix/ Alamy Stock Photo, p. 37 (disco); Directphoto Collection/ Alamy Stock Photo, p. 37 (punk); Michael Ochs Archives/ Getty Images, p. 37 (The Hustle); David E. Lucas/ Wikipedia, p. 38; George Gojkovich/ Getty Images, p. 39 (Erving); Wally McNamee/ Getty Images, p. 40 (Summer 1976); Fairchild Archive/ Getty Images, p. 40 (Summer 1972); STAFF/ Getty Images, p. 40 (Winter 1972); The Asahi Shimbun/ Getty Images, p. 41 (Olga Korbut); Popperfoto/ Getty Images, p. 41 (Pelé); Sovfoto/ Getty Images, p. 42 (1971); Robert LeRoy Knudsen/ Wikipedia, p. 43 (1973); Alain Machet (4)/ Alamy Stock Photo, p. 43 (March 1974); Ollie Atkins/ Wikipedia, p. 44 (1974); Rob Janoff/ Wikipedia, p. 44 (1976).